QUICK & EASY MEALS

•Cooking for Today•

QUICK & EASY MEALS

CAROLE HANDSLIP

Produced by Haldane Mason, London
for
Parragon
13 Whiteladies Road
Clifton
Bristol BS8 1PB

ISBN 0-75252-882-3

Printed in Italy

Reprinted in 1998

Art Direction: Ron Samuels
Editor: Vicky Hanson
Series Design: Pedro & Frances Prá-Lopez/Kingfisher Design
Page Design: Somewhere Creative
Photography & Styling: Amanda Heywood
Home Economist: Carole Handslip

Photographs on pages 6, 20, 34, 48 & 62 reproduced by permission of
ZEFA Picture Library (UK) Ltd

Note:
*Cup measurements in this book are for American cups. Tablespoons are assumed to be 15 ml.
Unless otherwise stated, milk is assumed to be full-fat, eggs are standard size 2 and
pepper is freshly ground black pepper.*

Contents

CHAPTER ONE

Soups & Salads

Soups are one of my favourite quick meals – so full of nourishment and so warming on a cold night. I remember arriving in Spain late one night after most of the cafés had closed. Tired and hungry, we persuaded one patron to set up a table and serve us a bowl of 'potaje'. It was wonderful; hot, tasty and thoroughly satisfying, containing almost every vegetable he had in the kitchen. The main ingredients were chick-peas (garbanzo beans) and tomatoes, and this has remained one of my favourite soups (see page 10). Served with chunks of crusty bread, it really is a meal in itself.

When making soups, remember that the better the stock, the better the soup. I use chicken stock for the basis of most of my soups as it works well with most ingredients but as an alternative keep the water you cook vegetables in – it makes a very good base.

Like the soups, the salads are substantial enough to form a meal in themselves – Hot Potato and Ham Salad (see page 15) will defeat even the largest appetites. The recipes in this section will serve four people as a main course or six as a starter.

Opposite: *Soups and salads are a good way to make the most of whatever vegetables are in season. Experiment with your own combinations.*

STEP 1

STEP 2

STEP 3

STEP 4

SMOKED FISH CHOWDER

A really substantial soup with a subtle smoky flavour, thick with chunks of fish and colourful vegetables.

SERVES: 4
PREPARATION: 10 MINS,
    COOKING: 15 MINS

90 g/ 3 oz streaky bacon, chopped
500 g/ 1 lb potatoes, diced finely
600 ml/ 1 pint/ 2½ cups milk
1 fresh bay leaf
425 g/ 14 oz can sweetcorn, drained
350 g/ 12 oz thin smoked haddock or cod fillet, skinned
4 spring onions (scallions), white and green parts, sliced thinly
salt and pepper
crusty bread to serve

1 Heat a large saucepan, add the bacon and dry-fry for 2 minutes, until the fat begins to run. Add the potatoes, milk, bay leaf and seasoning. Bring to the boil and simmer for 5 minutes.

2 Add the sweetcorn, fish and spring onions (scallions) and cook for a further 5 minutes.

3 Remove the fish with a perforated spoon and use 2 forks to break it into large flakes.

4 Return the fish to the soup and turn the soup into a soup tureen. Serve with chunks of crusty bread.

SMOKED FISH

I like to use natural oak-smoked fish rather than the bright yellow variety that has been dyed with colourings.
  The fishmonger will be very happy to skin the fish for you.

VARIATION

For a vegetarian alternative, omit the bacon and fish and use 250 g/8 oz cubed smoked tofu (bean curd) instead.

STEP 1

STEP 2

STEP 3

STEP 4

CHICK-PEA (GARBANZO BEAN) & TOMATO SOUP

A thick vegetable soup which is a delicious meal in itself. Serve with Parmesan cheese and warm ciabatta bread: one made with sun-dried tomatoes or spinach would go particularly well with the soup.

SERVES: 4
PREPARATION: **5** MINS,
  COOKING: **12** MINS

2 tbsp olive oil
2 leeks, sliced
2 courgettes (zucchini), diced
2 garlic cloves, crushed
2 x 425 g/14 oz cans chopped tomatoes
1 tbsp tomato purée (paste)
1 fresh bay leaf
900 ml/1½ pints/3½ cups chicken stock
425 g/14 oz can chick-peas (garbanzo beans), drained and rinsed
250 g/8 oz spinach
salt and pepper

TO SERVE:
Parmesan cheese
sun-dried tomato bread

1 Heat the oil in a large saucepan, add the leeks and courgettes (zucchini) and cook briskly for 5 minutes, stirring constantly.

2 Add the garlic, tomatoes, tomato purée (paste), bay leaf, stock and chick-peas (garbanzo beans). Bring to the boil and simmer for 5 minutes.

3 Shred the spinach finely, add to the soup and cook for 2 minutes. Season to taste.

4 Discard the bay leaf. Serve the soup with freshly grated Parmesan cheese and sun-dried tomato bread.

CHICK-PEAS (GARBANZO BEANS)

Chick-peas (garbanzo beans) are used extensively in North African cuisine and are also found in Spanish, Middle Eastern and Indian cooking. They have a nutty flavour with a firm texture and are an excellent canned product.

STEP 1

STEP 2

STEP 3

STEP 4

HUNGARIAN SAUSAGE SOUP

A rich, warming soup based on the famous Hungarian goulash, which is traditionally made with chunks of beef.

SERVES: 4
PREPARATION: 10 MINS,
    COOKING: 15–20 MINS

2 tbsp olive oil
2 onions, chopped
2 garlic cloves, chopped
1 tbsp paprika
500 g/ 1 lb potatoes, diced
1 red (bell) pepper, deseeded and chopped
425 g/ 14 oz can chopped tomatoes
1 tbsp tomato purée (paste)
2 tsp caraway seeds
1 fresh bay leaf
900 ml/ 1¹/₂ pints/ 3¹/₂ cups beef stock
175 g/ 6 oz kabanos sausage, sliced
2 tbsp chopped fresh parsley
4 tbsp soured cream
salt and pepper
chopped fresh parsley to garnish

1 Heat the oil in a saucepan and fry the onions over a high heat for 2 minutes. Add the garlic and paprika and fry briefly, stirring.

2 Add the potatoes, red (bell) pepper, tomatoes, tomato purée (paste), caraway seeds, bay leaf, stock and seasoning.

3 Cover and simmer for 10–15 minutes. Add the kabanos and parsley and cook for a further 2 minutes.

4 Pour the soup into warmed bowls and spoon a dollop of soured cream into each bowl. Garnish with parsley and serve at once.

PAPRIKA

Paprika is made from red capsicums which are dried and then ground to a powder. The paprika that is most widely available is the mild variety. Hot paprika, available from specialist shops, is also produced, although it is not as hot as chilli powder. Paprika is used extensively in Hungarian and Spanish cooking.

HOT POTATO & HAM SALAD

This is one of my favourite salads and a very adaptable one. With potatoes as a base you can vary the other ingredients, using egg, pickled herring or beetroot in place of the smoked ham.

STEP 1

SERVES: 4
PREPARATION: 10 MINS,
   COOKING: 8 MINS

175 g/6 oz smoked ham
500 g / 1 lb salad potatoes
6 spring onions (scallions), white and green
   parts, sliced
3 pickled dill cucumbers, halved and sliced
4 tbsp mayonnaise
4 tbsp thick natural yogurt
2 tbsp chopped fresh dill
salt and pepper

STEP 2

1 Cut the ham into 4 cm/1½ inch long strips.

2 Cut the potatoes into 1 cm/½ inch pieces and cook in boiling salted water for 8 minutes until tender.

3 Drain the potatoes and return to the pan with the spring onions (scallions), ham and cucumbers.

4 Combine the mayonnaise, yogurt, dill and seasoning and add to the pan. Stir until the potatoes are coated. Turn into a warmed dish and serve.

STEP 3

THICK YOGURT

Often sold as Greek or Greek-style yogurt, thick yogurt is rich and creamy with a fat content of about 10%. It is strained to concentrate the flavour, texture and fat content and for this reason it tastes sweeter than other natural yogurts. Because of its high fat content it does not curdle when heated, so it is useful to add to soups and sauces. It is also ideal to serve as a dessert with honey or to use instead of cream in fruit fools.

STEP 4

15

STEP 1

STEP 2

STEP 3

STEP 4

GOAT'S CHEESE SALAD

Hot melting goat's cheese on top of sliced tomato and basil with a base of hot ciabatta bread. The black olive vinaigrette and bitter salad leaves give a real tang to this dish – it's one of my favourite quick snacks.

SERVES: 4
PREPARATION: 15 MINS,
  COOKING: 5–6 MINS

3 tbsp olive oil
1 tbsp white wine vinegar
1 tsp black olive paste
1 garlic clove, crushed
1 tsp chopped fresh thyme
1 ciabatta loaf
4 small tomatoes, sliced
12 fresh basil leaves
2 x 125 g/4 oz logs goat's cheese
fresh basil sprigs to garnish
salad leaves to serve

1 Put the oil, vinegar, olive paste, garlic and thyme in a small bowl and whisk together.

2 Cut the ciabatta in half horizontally then in half vertically to make 4 pieces.

3 Drizzle some of the dressing over the bread then arrange the tomatoes and basil leaves on top.

4 Cut each log of goat's cheese into 6 slices and lay 3 slices on each piece of ciabatta.

5 Brush the cheese with some of the dressing and place in a preheated oven at 230°C/450°F/Gas Mark 8 for 5–6 minutes until turning brown at the edges.

6 Cut each piece of bread in half. Arrange the salad leaves on serving plates and top with the baked bread. Pour over the remaining dressing, garnish with basil sprigs and serve with salad leaves.

GOAT'S CHEESE

Goat's cheeses range in flavour from fresh and creamy to strong and tangy, developing flavour as they mature. They are made in a variety of shapes, usually rolls, rounds or pyramids and are generally fairly small. Fresh goat's cheese must be eaten within 2 days but the mature cheeses, which have a firmer, drier texture, will keep longer.

STEP 1

STEP 2

STEP 3

STEP 4

SWEET & SOUR TUNA SALAD

Flageolet (small navy) beans, courgettes (zucchini) and tomatoes are briefly cooked in a sweet and sour sauce, then allowed to cool before being mixed with flakes of tuna fish.

SERVES: **4**
PREPARATION: **10** MINS,
   COOKING: **10** MINS

2 tbsp olive oil
1 onion, chopped
2 garlic cloves, chopped
2 courgettes (zucchini), sliced
4 tomatoes, skinned
400 g/14 oz can flageolet (small navy)
  beans, drained and rinsed
10 black olives, pitted and halved
1 tbsp capers
1 tsp caster (superfine) sugar
1 tbsp wholegrain mustard
1 tbsp white wine vinegar
200 g/7 oz can tuna fish, drained
2 tbsp chopped fresh parsley
chopped fresh parsley to garnish
crusty bread to serve

1 Heat the oil in a frying pan (skillet) and fry the onion and garlic for 5 minutes until soft. Add the courgettes (zucchini) and cook for 3 minutes, stirring occasionally.

2 Cut the tomatoes in half then into thin wedges.

3 Add the tomatoes to the pan with the beans, olives, capers, sugar,

mustard and vinegar. Simmer for 2 minutes, stirring gently, then allow to cool slightly.

4 Flake the tuna fish and stir into the bean mixture with the parsley. Garnish with parsley and serve lukewarm with crusty bread.

CAPERS

Capers are the flower buds of the caper bush, which is native to the Mediterranean region. Capers are preserved in vinegar and salt and give a distinctive flavour to this salad. They are much used in Italian and Provençal cooking.

18

CHAPTER TWO

Pasta, Grains & Pulses

Grains and pulses form the basis of many of the world's most exciting and popular recipes. They are nutritious, provide dietary fibre and add a variety of textures and flavours to a great many dishes. A good store of these versatile ingredients is indispensable for quick and easy meals. Pulses are one of the few canned foods worth buying; they're good to eat and easy to use at a moment's notice, avoiding the soaking and boiling necessary to prepare dried beans and peas.

Basmati rice, the most fragrant of rices, cooks in only 8 minutes, so is perfect for the cook in a hurry. Bulgur wheat and couscous make delicious changes from rice as accompaniments and, as they are both precooked, they only need to be soaked in boiling water before being fluffed up with a fork.

Pasta must be the most marvellous quick food – both nourishing and satisfying. Fresh pasta, which comes in so many different flavours and shapes, takes only 3–4 minutes to cook, but even dried pasta is ready in 10–12 minutes.

Opposite: *A variety of pastas should be in every cook's store cupboard: with a quick sauce, they will provide a satisfying meal in a matter of minutes.*

STEP 1

STEP 2

STEP 4

STEP 6

LAMB COUSCOUS

Couscous is a speciality in many North African countries and is usually accompanied by a spicy mixture of meat or sausage and some kind of fruit. Here I've used fresh dates and raisins.

SERVES: 4
PREPARATION: 10 MINS,
  COOKING: 25 MINS

2 tbsp olive oil
500 g/ 1 lb lamb fillet (tenderloin), sliced
  thinly
2 onions, sliced
2 garlic cloves, chopped
1 cinnamon stick
1 tsp ground ginger
1 tsp paprika
1/2 tsp chilli powder
600 ml/ 1 pint/ 2 1/2 cups hot chicken stock
3 carrots, sliced thinly
2 turnips, halved and sliced
425 g/ 14 oz can chopped tomatoes
30 g/ 1 oz/ 2 tbsp raisins
425 g/ 14 oz can chick-peas (garbanzo
  beans), drained and rinsed
3 courgettes (zucchini), sliced
125 g/ 4 oz fresh dates, halved and pitted or
  125 g/ 4 oz dried apricots
300 g/ 10 oz/ 1 3/4 cups couscous
600 ml/ 1 pint/ 2 1/2 cups boiling water
salt

1 Heat the oil in a frying pan (skillet) and fry the lamb briskly for 3 minutes until browned. Remove the meat from the pan with a perforated spoon or fish slice and set aside.

2 Add the onions to the pan and cook, stirring, until soft. Add the garlic and spices and cook for 1 minute.

3 Add the stock, carrots, turnips, tomatoes, raisins, chick-peas (garbanzo beans) and lamb. Cover, bring to the boil and simmer for 12 minutes.

4 Add the courgettes (zucchini), dates or apricots and season with salt. Cover again and cook for 8 minutes.

5 Meanwhile, put the couscous in a bowl with 1 teaspoon of salt and pour over the boiling water. Leave to soak for 5 minutes, then fluff with a fork.

6 To serve, pile the couscous on to a warmed serving platter and make a hollow in the centre. Put the meat and vegetables in the hollow and pour over some of the sauce. Serve the rest of the sauce separately.

COUSCOUS

Traditionally couscous is steamed in a couscousière, a type of colander that sits over the stew. I find it easier to soak it in boiling water then fluff it up with a fork.

STEP 1

STEP 2

STEP 3

STEP 4

VEGETABLE CURRY

Vegetables cooked in a mildly spiced curry sauce with yogurt and fresh coriander (cilantro) stirred in just before serving.

SERVES: 4
PREPARATION: 10 MINS,
    COOKING: 25 MINS

2 tbsp sunflower oil
1 onion, sliced
2 tsp cumin seeds
2 tbsp ground coriander
1 tsp ground turmeric
2 tsp ground ginger
1 tsp chopped fresh red chilli
2 garlic cloves, chopped
425 g/14 oz can chopped tomatoes
3 tbsp powdered coconut mixed with
    300 ml/^{1}/$_2$ pint/1^1/$_4$ cups boiling water
1 small cauliflower, broken into florets
2 courgettes (zucchini), sliced
2 carrots, sliced
1 potato, diced
425 g/14 oz can chick-peas (garbanzo
    beans), drained and rinsed
150 ml/^{1}/$_4$ pint/^{2}/$_3$ cup thick yogurt
2 tbsp mango chutney
3 tbsp chopped fresh coriander (cilantro)
salt and pepper
fresh coriander (cilantro) sprigs to garnish

TO SERVE:
Onion Relish (see page 79)
Banana Raita (see page 79)
basmati rice
naan bread

1 Heat the oil in a saucepan and fry the onion until softened. Add the cumin, ground coriander, turmeric, ginger, chilli and garlic and fry for 1 minute.

2 Add the tomatoes and coconut mixture and mix well.

3 Add the cauliflower, courgettes (zucchini), carrots, potato, chick-peas (garbanzo beans) and seasoning. Cover and simmer for 20 minutes until the vegetables are tender.

4 Stir in the yogurt, mango chutney and fresh coriander (cilantro) and heat through gently, but do not boil. Garnish with coriander (cilantro) sprigs and serve with onion relish, banana raita, basmati rice and naan bread.

STEP 1

STEP 2

STEP 3

STEP 4

DUCK BREAST WITH BEANS

Succulent slices of duck breast served with a selection of beans cooked with bacon, wine and herbs. An unusual and delicious combination of flavours.

SERVES: 4–6
PREPARATION: 15 MINS,
   COOKING: 15 MINS

4–6 duck breasts, about 175 g/6 oz each
2 tbsp olive oil
1 onion, chopped
2 garlic cloves, chopped
125 g/4 oz streaky bacon, chopped
300 ml/½ pint/1¼ cups red wine
2 tbsp tomato purée (paste)
2 tsp clear honey
1 fresh bay leaf
1 tbsp chopped fresh marjoram
425 g/14 oz can pinto beans or red kidney
   beans, drained and rinsed
425 g/14 oz can haricot (navy) beans,
   drained and rinsed
425 g/14 oz can flageolet (small navy)
   beans, drained and rinsed
425 g/14 oz can green lentils, drained and
   rinsed
1 tbsp balsamic vinegar
2 tbsp chopped fresh parsley
salt and pepper
fresh marjoram sprigs to garnish
green salad to serve

1 Prick the skin of the duck breasts then put the breasts skin side down on a rack in a grill (broiler) pan. Brush with oil and cook under a preheated moderate grill (broiler) for 3–4 minutes. Turn the duck over and grill (broil) for a further 5–10 minutes until most of the fat has run out, the skin is crisp, but the flesh is still pink.

2 Meanwhile, heat the remaining oil in a heavy-based saucepan and fry the onion, garlic and bacon, stirring occasionally, for 5 minutes.

3 Add the wine, tomato purée (paste), honey, bay leaf, marjoram, beans, lentils and seasoning. Bring to the boil and simmer for 5 minutes. Stir in the vinegar and parsley, adding a little extra wine or water if necessary.

4 Slice the duck breasts and divide between warmed serving plates. Spoon some beans and lentils next to the duck. Garnish with marjoram sprigs and serve with a green salad.

DUCK BREASTS

Duck breasts vary in size depending on the breed. If the breasts are large you will only need 2 to serve 4 people, but remember they will take longer to cook.

TOMATO & COURGETTE (ZUCCHINI) FRITTATA

A frittata is a type of Italian omelette, thick with a variety of vegetables, fish or meat. You can add almost anything to the eggs. It is also delicious eaten cold (but not chilled) and makes an ideal picnic dish.

STEP 1

SERVES: 4
PREPARATION: 10 MINS,
   COOKING: 20 MINS

3 tbsp olive oil
1 onion, chopped
2 garlic cloves, chopped
250 g/8 oz courgettes (zucchini), sliced
   thinly
4 eggs
425 g/14 oz can borlotti beans, drained and
   rinsed
3 tomatoes, skinned and chopped
2 tbsp chopped fresh chives
1 tbsp chopped fresh basil
60 g/2 oz/¹/₂ cup grated Gruyère (Swiss)
   cheese
salt and pepper

1 Heat 2 tablespoons of the oil in a frying pan (skillet) and fry the onion and garlic, stirring occasionally, until soft. Add the courgettes (zucchini) and cook until softened.

2 Break the eggs into a bowl and add the seasoning, fried vegetables, beans, tomatoes and herbs.

3 Heat the remaining oil in a 24 cm/9½ inch omelette pan, add the egg mixture and fry gently for

STEP 2

5 minutes until the eggs have almost set and the underside is brown.

4 Sprinkle the cheese over the top and place the pan under a preheated moderate grill (broiler) for 3–4 minutes until set on the top but still moist in the middle. Cut into wedges and serve warm or at room temperature.

STEP 3

GRUYERE (SWISS) CHEESE

This famous cheese is made from unpasteurized cow's milk and has a sweet, nutty flavour, which enhances the taste of this frittata. Gruyère (Swiss) cheese is firm and close textured and has small holes interspersed throughout.

STEP 4

STEP 1

STEP 2

STEP 3

STEP 4

PASTA PROVENÇALE

A Mediterranean mixture of red (bell) peppers, garlic and courgettes (zucchini) cooked in olive oil and tossed with pasta. The Gruyère (Swiss) cheese topping is grilled (broiled) until brown and bubbling.

SERVES: 4
PREPARATION: 10 MINS,
  COOKING: 20 MINS

3 tbsp olive oil
1 onion, sliced
2 garlic cloves, chopped
3 red (bell) peppers, deseeded and cut into
  strips
3 courgettes (zucchini), sliced
425 g/14 oz can chopped tomatoes
3 tbsp sun-dried tomato paste
2 tbsp chopped fresh basil
250 g/8 oz fresh pasta spirals
125 g/4 oz/1 cup grated Gruyère (Swiss)
  cheese
salt and pepper
fresh basil sprigs to garnish

1 Heat the oil in a heavy-based saucepan or flameproof casserole. Add the onion and garlic and cook, stirring occasionally, until softened. Add the (bell) peppers and courgettes (zucchini) and fry for 5 minutes, stirring occasionally.

2 Add the tomatoes, sun-dried tomato paste, basil and seasoning, cover and cook for a further 5 minutes.

3 Meanwhile, bring a large saucepan of salted water to the boil and add the pasta. Stir and bring back to the boil. Reduce the heat slightly and cook, uncovered, for 3 minutes, until just tender. Drain thoroughly and add to the vegetables. Toss gently to mix well.

4 Put the mixture into a shallow ovenproof dish and sprinkle over the cheese.

5 Cook under a preheated grill (broiler) for 5 minutes until the cheese is golden brown. Garnish with basil sprigs and serve.

FRESH PASTA

Be careful not to overcook fresh pasta – it should be 'al dente' (retaining some bite). It takes only a few minutes to cook as it is still full of moisture.

STEP 1

STEP 3

STEP 4

STEP 5

PASTA WITH BROCCOLI

Broccoli coated in a garlic-flavoured cream sauce, served on herb tagliatelle. Try sprinkling with toasted pine nuts to add extra crunch.

SERVES: 4
PREPARATION: 5 MINS,
  COOKING: 5 MINS

500 g/ 1 lb broccoli
300 g/ 10 oz/ 1¼ cups garlic & herb cream
  cheese
4 tbsp milk
350 g/ 12 oz fresh herb tagliatelle
30 g/ 1 oz/¼ cup grated Parmesan cheese
chopped fresh chives to garnish

1 Cut the broccoli into even-sized florets. Cook the broccoli in boiling salted water for 3 minutes and drain thoroughly.

2 Put the soft cheese into a saucepan and heat gently, stirring, until melted. Add the milk and stir until well combined.

3 Add the broccoli to the cheese mixture and stir to coat.

4 Meanwhile, bring a large saucepan of salted water to the boil and add the tagliatelle. Stir and bring back to the boil. Reduce the heat slightly and cook the tagliatelle, uncovered, for 3–4 minutes until just tender.

5 Drain the tagliatelle thoroughly and divide among 4 warmed serving plates. Spoon the sauce on top. Sprinkle with grated Parmesan cheese, garnish with chives and serve.

PASTA

A herb flavoured pasta goes particularly well with the broccoli sauce, but failing this, a tagliatelle verde or 'paglia e fieno' (literally 'straw and hay' – thin green and yellow noodles) will fit the bill.

CHAPTER THREE

Fish & Shellfish

Fish is an excellent choice for a quick meal: not only does it cook quickly, if you ask the fishmonger to scale, gut and fillet the fish, this will save you time-consuming preparation in the kitchen. Many fish, especially flat fish such as sole or plaice, can be grilled (broiled) or fried whole. For an even quicker meal, cut the fillets into strips and poach them in a little milk or wine before thickening it into a sauce.

Monkfish, salmon or other firm-fleshed fish can be cubed and threaded on to skewers. Fish kebabs need to be cooked quickly, so preheat the grill (broiler) to the hottest setting to ensure the fish chars on the outside but stays succulent and moist inside.

The essential characteristic of all fish or shellfish is the delicacy of flavour and texture. Take great care not to spoil them by overcooking, which makes the flesh dry and tough.

Opposite: *Shellfish take very little time to cook but make all kinds of exotic meals.*

STEP 1

STEP 2

STEP 3

STEP 5

THAI PRAWN (SHRIMP) STIR-FRY

A very quick and tasty stir-fry using prawns (shrimp) and cucumber, cooked with the traditional flavourings of Thai cuisine – lemon grass, chilli and ginger.

SERVES: 4
PREPARATION: 15 MINS,
  COOKING: 5 MINS

$^1/_2$ cucumber
2 tbsp sunflower oil
6 spring onions (scallions), halved
    lengthways and cut into 4 cm/1$^1/_2$ inch
    lengths
1 stalk lemon grass, sliced thinly
1 garlic clove, chopped
1 tsp chopped fresh red chilli
125 g/4 oz oyster mushrooms
1 tsp chopped ginger root
350 g/12 oz cooked peeled prawns (shrimp)
2 tsp cornflour (cornstarch)
2 tbsp water
1 tbsp dark soy sauce
$^1/_2$ tsp fish sauce
2 tbsp dry sherry or rice wine
boiled rice to serve

1 Cut the cucumber into strips about 5 mm x 4 cm/$^1/_4$ x 1$^3/_4$ inches.

2 Heat the oil in a wok or large frying pan (skillet), add the spring onions (scallions), cucumber, lemon grass, garlic, chilli, mushrooms and ginger and stir-fry for 2 minutes.

3 Add the prawns (shrimp) and stir-fry for a further minute.

4 Mix together the cornflour (cornstarch), water, soy sauce and fish sauce until smooth.

5 Stir the cornflour (cornstarch) mixture and dry sherry or rice wine into the pan and heat through, stirring, until the sauce has thickened. Serve immediately with boiled rice.

LEMON GRASS

Lemon grass is used extensively in South-East Asian cooking, particularly that of Thailand. You can thinly slice the white part of the stem and leave it in the cooked dish, or use the whole stem and remove it before serving. You can buy lemon grass chopped and dried, or preserved in jars, but neither has the fragrance or delicacy of the fresh variety.

STEP 1

STEP 2

STEP 3

STEP 4

SCALLOPS WITH MIXED MUSHROOMS

Scallops have a rich but delicate flavour. When sautéed with oyster mushrooms and bathed in brandy and cream, they make a really special dinner for two.

SERVES: 2
PREPARATION: 5 MINS,
  COOKING: 5 MINS

15 g/½ oz/1 tbsp butter
250 g/8 oz shelled queen scallops
1 tbsp olive oil
50 g/2 oz oyster mushrooms, sliced
50 g/2 oz shiitake mushrooms, sliced
1 garlic clove, chopped
4 spring onions (scallions), white and green
  parts, sliced
3 tbsp double (heavy) cream
1 tbsp brandy
salt and pepper
sprigs of fresh dill to garnish
basmati rice to serve

1 Heat the butter in a heavy-based frying pan (skillet) and fry the scallops for 1 minute, turning occasionally, then remove from the pan with a perforated spoon and keep warm.

2 Add the oil to the pan and heat. Add the mushrooms, garlic and spring onions (scallions) and cook for 2 minutes, stirring constantly.

3 Return the scallops to the pan. Add the cream and brandy. Season to taste and heat gently to warm through.

4 Garnish with dill sprigs and serve with basmati rice.

SCALLOPS

Scallops, which consist of a large, round white muscle with a bright orange roe, are the most delicious seafood in the prettiest of shells. The rounded half of the shell can be used as a dish in which to serve the scallops. The shells can grow to about 18 cm/7 inches across.

  Small queen scallops, or queenies, are only about 7 cm/3 inches across and are usually sold ready-prepared, both fresh and frozen, sometimes without the roe.

BUTTERFLY PRAWNS

In my view this is the best way to eat giant prawns – simply fried with chilli and lots of garlic.

STEP 1

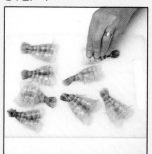

STEP 2

STEP 3

STEP 5

SERVES: 4
PREPARATION: 5 MINS,
  COOKING: 10 MINS

20 raw tiger prawns
chilli powder for sprinkling
4 garlic cloves
120 ml/4 fl oz/¹/₂ cup olive oil
salt
fresh flat-leaf parsley sprigs to garnish
crusty bread to serve

1 Make a cut along the underside of each prawn, being careful not to cut right through the shell.

2 Place the prawns shell side up on a board and press firmly to crack the shells and flatten the prawns. Remove any black intestinal threads that run along the back.

3 Sprinkle the flesh with salt and chilli powder to taste.

4 Cut the garlic cloves into quarters and put in a large frying pan (skillet) with the oil, then heat until the garlic is just turning pale gold.

5 Place a few prawns in the pan, shell side down, and cook for 2–3 minutes. Turn over and cook for a further 1–2 minutes. Remove with a perforated spoon and keep warm while cooking the remainder.

6 Arrange the prawns on warmed serving plates. Pour over the oil and garlic, garnish with flat-leaf parsley and serve with lots of crusty bread to dip in the flavoured oil.

TIGER PRAWNS

Be sure to buy raw prawns for this recipe. I like green tiger prawns or freshwater king (jumbo) prawns. Both are available with the heads already removed. Generally speaking, prawns from colder waters have a better flavour than those from warmer waters such as the Mediterranean.

STEP 1

STEP 3

STEP 4

STEP 6

SALMON FILLETS WITH CAPER SAUCE

The richness of salmon is beautifully balanced by the tangy capers in this creamy herb sauce.

SERVES: **4**
PREPARATION: **5 MINS,**
  COOKING: **20 MINS**

4 salmon fillets, skinned
1 fresh bay leaf
few black peppercorns
1 tsp white wine vinegar
150 ml/^{1}/$_4$ pint/^{2}/$_3$ cup fish stock
3 tbsp double (heavy) cream
1 tbsp capers
1 tbsp chopped fresh dill
1 tbsp chopped fresh chives
1 tsp cornflour (cornstarch)
2 tbsp milk
salt and pepper
new potatoes to serve

TO GARNISH:
fresh dill sprigs
chive flowers

1 Lay the salmon fillets in a shallow ovenproof dish. Add the bay leaf, peppercorns, vinegar and stock.

2 Cover with foil and bake in a preheated oven at 180°C/350°F/ Gas Mark 4 for 15–20 minutes until the flesh is opaque and flakes easily when tested with a fork.

3 Transfer the fish to warmed serving plates, cover and keep warm.

4 Strain the cooking liquid into a saucepan. Stir in the cream, capers, herbs and seasoning to taste.

5 Blend the cornflour (cornstarch) with the milk. Add to the saucepan and heat, stirring, until thickened slightly. Boil for 1 minute.

6 Spoon the sauce over the salmon, garnish with dill sprigs and chive flowers and serve with new potatoes.

LOW-FAT VERSION

If you want to cut down on fat and calories, use fromage frais or thick yogurt instead of the cream and omit the cornflour (cornstarch) and milk. Don't allow the sauce to boil.

SALMON

Ask the fishmonger to skin the fillets for you. The cooking time for the salmon will depend on the thickness of the fish: the thin tail end of the salmon takes the least time to cook.

STEP 1

STEP 2

STEP 4

STEP 6

MONKFISH KEBABS

I like to serve monkfish kebabs grilled (broiled) until charred on the outside but still moist on the inside. Other firm fish, such as salmon, swordfish or halibut, can be used instead of monkfish.

SERVES: 4
PREPARATION: 5 MINS,
   COOKING: 12 MINS

750 g/1½ lb monkfish tail
3 tbsp olive oil
2 garlic cloves, crushed
2 tbsp powdered coconut
120 ml/4 fl oz/½ cup boiling water
1 tsp ground coriander
½ tsp ground cumin
1 tsp ground turmeric
1 tsp ground ginger
3 tbsp double (heavy) cream
1 tbsp chopped fresh coriander (cilantro)

1 Remove the central bone from the fish and cut the fish into 2.5 cm/ 1 inch cubes. Put in a bowl with the oil and garlic and mix until the fish is coated.

2 Remove the fish from the oil and garlic mixture and thread on to 8 wooden skewers. Set aside.

3 Blend the powdered coconut with the boiling water. Heat the oil and garlic mixture in a saucepan, add the spices and cook, stirring, for 30 seconds. Add the coconut mixture and boil for 5 minutes.

4 Add the cream and chopped coriander (cilantro) and boil for 1 minute.

5 Put the fish under a preheated hot grill (broiler) and cook for 5–6 minutes, turning once, until charred outside but still moist on the inside.

6 Arrange 2 kebabs on each warmed serving plate, pour over the sauce and serve.

MONKFISH

Monkfish has a single narrow, vertical bone along the back, and no other bones. The flesh is covered with a tough transparent membrane which should be removed before cooking. Ask the fishmonger to prepare the fish for you if you like.

SKEWERS

Soak the wooden skewers in water for 5 minutes before use to prevent them burning under the grill (broiler).

STEP 1

STEP 2

STEP 3

STEP 4

PLAICE FILLETS WITH GRAPES

Fish is ideal for a quick meal, especially when cut into strips as in this recipe: it takes only minutes to cook. You could use salmon or lemon sole if you prefer.

SERVES: 4
PREPARATION: 10 MINS,
    COOKING: 8 MINS

500 g/1 lb plaice fillets, skinned
4 spring onions (scallions), white and green parts, sliced diagonally
120 ml/4 fl oz/$\frac{1}{2}$ cup dry white wine
1 tbsp cornflour (cornstarch)
2 tbsp milk
2 tbsp chopped fresh dill
50 ml/2 fl oz/$\frac{1}{4}$ cup double (heavy) cream
125 g/4 oz seedless white (green) grapes
1 tsp lemon juice
salt and pepper
fresh dill sprigs to garnish

TO SERVE:
basmati rice
courgette ribbons

1 Cut the fish into strips about 5 mm x 4 cm/$\frac{1}{4}$ x 1$\frac{3}{4}$ inches and put into a frying pan (skillet) with the spring onions (scallions), wine and seasoning.

2 Bring to the boil, cover and simmer for 4 minutes. Carefully transfer the fish to a warmed serving dish. Cover and keep warm.

3 Mix together the cornflour (cornstarch) and milk then add to the pan with the dill and cream. Bring to the boil and boil, stirring, for 2 minutes until thickened.

4 Add the grapes and lemon juice and heat through very gently for 1–2 minutes, then pour over the fish. Garnish with dill and serve with basmati rice and courgette ribbons.

DILL

Dill has a fairly strong aniseed flavour that goes very well with fish. The feathery leaves are particularly attractive when used as a garnish. Dill is widely used in Scandinavian dishes such as gravadlax, and is often paired with cucumber.

CHAPTER FOUR

Meat & Poultry

Generally, meat available in supermarkets is stripped of most of its fat and cut into fillets, stir-fry strips, goujons, escalopes and many other shapes and sizes, all ready to use. This reduces wastage and saves your time. The dishes in this chapter offer many options for quick meals made with different meats and cooking methods.

Chicken is the most versatile of ingredients for quick cooking and is very low in fat compared to red meats. I prefer to use free-range chicken whenever possible as the flavour is definitely better than that of the intensively reared bird.

Venison also makes a delicious and healthy alternative to red meats, with a rich gamey flavour yet low fat content. It is excellent served with a sharp, fruity sauce such as Venison with Plums (see page 58).

Opposite: *Cattle and sheep graze in the rugged hills of Colorado.*

TOMATO & CHORIZO PIZZA

Spicy chorizo sausage blends beautifully with juicy tomatoes and mild, melting Mozzarella cheese. This pizza makes a delicious light lunch served with a crisp green salad.

STEP 1

STEP 2

STEP 3

STEP 4

SERVES: 2
PREPARATION: 10 MINS,
    COOKING: 15 MINS

23 cm/9 inch pizza base
1 tbsp black olive paste
1 tbsp olive oil
1 onion, sliced
1 garlic clove, crushed
4 tomatoes, sliced
75 g/3 oz chorizo sausage, sliced
1 tsp chopped fresh oregano
125 g/4 oz Mozzarella cheese, sliced
6 black olives, pitted and halved
black pepper

1 Put the pizza base on a baking sheet and spread the black olive paste to within 1 cm/½ inch of the edge.

2 Heat the oil in a frying pan (skillet) and cook the onion for 2 minutes. Add the garlic and cook for 1 minute.

3 Spread the onion mixture over the pizza base and arrange the tomato and chorizo slices on top.

4 Sprinkle with the oregano, season with black pepper and arrange the Mozzarella cheese and olives on top.

5 Bake in a preheated oven at 230°C/450°F/Gas Mark 8 for 10 minutes until the cheese is melted and golden. Serve immediately.

PIZZA BASES

There are several varieties of pizza base available. I prefer the ones with added olive oil because the dough is much lighter and tastier.

STEP 1

STEP 3

STEP 4

STEP 5

CHICKEN CHOW MEIN

A quick stir-fry of chicken and vegetables which are mixed with Chinese egg noodles and a dash of sesame oil.

SERVES: 4
PREPARATION: 10 MINS,
  COOKING: 6 MINS

250 g/8 oz thread egg noodles
175 g/6 oz broccoli florets
3 tbsp sunflower oil
1 garlic clove, sliced
2.5 cm/1 inch piece ginger root, peeled and
  chopped
250 g/8 oz chicken fillet, sliced thinly
1 onion, sliced
125 g/4 oz shiitake mushrooms, sliced
1 red (bell) pepper, deseeded and cut into
  thin strips
1 tsp cornflour (cornstarch)
2 tbsp water
425 g/14 oz can baby sweetcorn, drained
  and halved
2 tbsp dry sherry
2 tbsp soy sauce
1 tsp sesame oil
2 tbsp sesame seeds, toasted

1 Put the noodles in a bowl, cover with boiling water and leave to stand for 4 minutes. Drain thoroughly.

2 Meanwhile, blanch the broccoli in boiling salted water for 2 minutes, then drain.

3 Heat the oil in a wok or large frying pan (skillet), add the garlic, ginger, chicken and onion and stir-fry for 2 minutes until the chicken is golden and the onion softened.

4 Add the broccoli, mushrooms and red (bell) pepper and stir-fry for a further 2 minutes.

5 Mix the cornflour (cornstarch) with the water then stir into the pan with the baby sweetcorn, sherry, soy sauce, drained noodles and sesame oil and cook, stirring, until the sauce is thickened and the noodles warmed through. Sprinkle with the sesame seeds and serve.

SESAME SEEDS

Sesame seeds are packed with vitamins, calcium, iron and protein, as well as having a delicious flavour, especially when toasted. Put them in a heavy-based frying pan (skillet) and cook for 2–3 minutes until they turn brown and begin to pop. Cover the pan so the seeds don't jump out and shake constantly to prevent them burning.

STEP 1

STEP 2

STEP 3

STEP 4

BEEF STROGANOFF

A combination of beef, mushrooms and onion laced with a sauce of double (heavy) cream and brandy.

SERVES: 4
PREPARATION: 10 MINS,
    COOKING: 6 MINS

*500 g/1 lb sirloin steak slices, about 5 mm/
    ¼ inch thick*
2 tbsp olive oil
250 g/8 oz chestnut mushrooms, sliced
1 garlic clove, chopped
*1 bunch spring onions (scallions), white and
    green parts, cut into strips*
*150 ml/¼ pint/⅔ cup double (heavy)
    cream*
2 tbsp brandy
salt and pepper
fresh flat-leaf parsley sprigs to garnish

TO SERVE:
basmati rice and wild rice
green salad

1 Cut the meat across the grain into 5 mm x 4 cm/¼ x 1¾ inch strips.

2 Heat 1 tablespoon of the oil in a heavy-based frying pan (skillet) or wok, add the meat and stir-fry for 2 minutes until the meat is browned. Remove from the pan with a perforated spoon and keep warm.

3 Add the remaining oil to the pan then stir-fry the mushrooms, garlic and spring onions (scallions) for 2 minutes.

4 Return the meat to the pan with the cream, brandy and seasoning to taste and heat gently to warm through.

5 Garnish with flat-leaf parsley and serve with basmati rice and wild rice and a green salad.

SIRLOIN STEAK

Cut the meat across the grain so that there will be less shrinkage when it is cooked. Make sure the oil is very hot when you add the meat so that it browns and seals as soon as it touches the pan.

PORK WITH MUSTARD CREAM SAUCE

The thinner the meat the less time it will take to cook. You could use the same recipe for turkey fillet or escalope of veal, if you prefer.

SERVES: 4
PREPARATION: 5 MINS,
    COOKING: 12 MINS

2 tbsp olive oil
4 escalopes of pork, 150–175 g/5–6 oz
    each
1 garlic clove, chopped
6 spring onions (scallions), white and green
    parts, sliced diagonally
120 ml/4 fl oz/¹/₂ cup dry white wine
1 tsp chopped fresh sage
2 tsp cornflour (cornstarch)
2 tbsp milk
2 tbsp Meaux mustard
75 ml/3 fl oz/¹/₃ cup double (heavy) cream
salt and pepper
fresh sage sprigs to garnish
fresh herb noodles to serve

1 Heat the oil in a heavy-based frying pan (skillet) and fry the pork on one side for 1–2 minutes until just turning brown, then turn and fry the other side for 1–2 minutes.

2 Add the garlic and spring onions (scallions) and fry for 1 minute.

3 Pour in the wine, add the sage and seasoning, then cover and cook for 4 minutes.

4 Mix together the cornflour (cornstarch) and milk and stir into the pan. Stir in the mustard then the cream and boil, stirring, for 2 minutes until thickened.

5 Garnish with sage sprigs and serve with fresh herb noodles.

MEAUX MUSTARD

This delicious mustard from France is made from brown and white mustard seeds and has a grainy texture with a warm spicy flavour. Do not keep for more than 3 months as it will begin to darken and dry out.

STEP 1

STEP 2

STEP 3

STEP 4

STEP 1

STEP 2

STEP 3

STEP 4

VENISON WITH PLUMS

The rich, slightly gamey flavour of venison is complemented by fruit such as plums, cranberries or redcurrants. Add a little port and brandy and you have a delectable sauce.

SERVES: 4
PREPARATION: 10 MINS,
   COOKING: 10 MINS

500 g/1 lb venison fillet (tenderloin)
2 tbsp olive oil
4 plums, halved, pitted and sliced
1 tsp chopped fresh sage
6 spring onions (scallions), white and green
   parts, cut into 2.5 cm/1 inch lengths
1 tbsp cornflour (cornstarch)
2 tbsp orange juice
150 ml/¹/₄ pint/²/₃ cup stock
4 tbsp port
1 tbsp redcurrant jelly
1 tbsp brandy
salt and pepper
fresh purple sage sprigs to garnish
creamed potatoes to serve

1 Cut the venison into 1 cm/¹/₂ inch strips. Heat the oil in a heavy-based frying pan (skillet) and fry the venison over a high heat for about 2 minutes until browned. Remove from the pan with a perforated spoon.

2 Add the plums, sage and spring onions (scallions) to the pan and cook for 2 minutes, stirring occasionally.

3 Mix the cornflour (cornstarch) with the orange juice and add to the pan. Add the stock, port and redcurrant jelly and heat, stirring, until thickened.

4 Return the venison to the pan, season to taste and pour in the brandy. Heat gently to warm through. Garnish with purple sage and serve with creamed potatoes.

VENISON

Venison is a fine-textured, dark red meat with very little fat, which makes it a healthy option. If venison is eaten young it is very tender, and better cuts such as saddle or loin can be roasted, but do not overcook them – they should still be fairly pink inside.

STEP 1

STEP 2

STEP 3

STEP 4

LAMB & GINGER STIR-FRY

Slices of lamb cooked with garlic, ginger and shiitake mushrooms make a quick and easy supper. I prefer this dish when served with Chinese egg noodles, but plain boiled rice is also a good accompaniment. Substitute beef or pork strips for the lamb for a change.

SERVES: 4
PREPARATION: 10 MINS,
    COOKING: 6 MINS

500 g/1 lb lamb fillet (tenderloin)
2 tbsp sunflower oil
1 tbsp chopped ginger root
2 garlic cloves, chopped
6 spring onions (scallions), white and green
    parts, diagonally sliced
175 g/6 oz shiitake mushrooms, sliced
175 g/6 oz sugar snap peas
1 tsp cornflour (cornstarch)
2 tbsp dry sherry
1 tbsp light soy sauce
1 tsp sesame oil
1 tbsp sesame seeds, toasted (see page 52)
Chinese egg noodles to serve

1 Cut the lamb into 5 mm/¼ inch slices.

2 Heat the oil in a wok or frying pan (skillet). Add the lamb and stir-fry for 2 minutes.

3 Add the ginger, garlic, spring onions (scallions), mushrooms and sugar snap peas and stir-fry for 2 minutes.

4 Blend the cornflour (cornstarch) with the sherry and stir into the wok. Add the soy sauce and sesame oil and cook, stirring, for 1 minute until thickened. Sprinkle over the sesame seeds and serve with Chinese egg noodles.

SHIITAKE MUSHROOMS

An Oriental mushroom much used in Chinese and Japanese cooking. Shiitake mushrooms have a slightly meaty flavour and can be bought both fresh and dried. Their powerful flavour will permeate more bland mushrooms so they are excellent used in conjunction with button mushrooms. Cook them briefly or they begin to toughen.

CHAPTER FIVE

Desserts

Here are some wonderful ways to finish your meal. They are all very quick, and although they are mainly meant for everyday meals, they look sufficiently stunning for a special dinner.

Fruit is always the obvious choice for a simple sweet course but make sure the fruit is ripe when you serve it, or it will not be juicy and its flavour will not be fully developed. A ripe fruit should smell fragrant.

There's always enough time to make a pudding, however rushed you are – here are a few more quick ideas. Sprinkle soft brown sugar over a little dish of fromage frais for a popular French dish; drop some raspberries or strawberries into a glass of red or white wine; stir some crushed berries into a bowl of thick natural yogurt to make a quick fool; slice a mango, cover with whipped cream, sprinkle with demerara (brown crystal) sugar and grill (broil) until caramelized; fry bananas in butter and sugar, then flame with a tot of rum.

Opposite: *Fresh fruit needs little preparation to be turned into a delicious dessert.*

STEP 1

STEP 2

STEP 3

STEP 6

QUICK TIRAMISU

This quick version of one of the most popular Italian desserts is ready in minutes. I first tasted this delicious creamy dessert in a little restaurant in San Gimignano, overlooking the cypress trees of Tuscany.

SERVES: 4
PREPARATION: 10 MINS

250 g/8 oz/1 cup Mascarpone or full-fat
   soft cheese
1 egg, separated
2 tbsp natural yogurt
2 tbsp caster (superfine) sugar
2 tbsp dark rum
2 tbsp strong black coffee
8 sponge fingers (lady-fingers)
2 tbsp grated dark chocolate

1 Put the cheese in a bowl, add the egg yolk and yogurt and beat until smooth.

2 Whisk the egg white until stiff but not dry, then whisk in the sugar and carefully fold into the cheese mixture.

3 Spoon half the mixture into 4 sundae glasses.

4 Mix together the rum and coffee in a shallow dish. Dip the sponge fingers (lady-fingers) into the rum mixture, break them in half, or into smaller pieces if necessary, and divide among the glasses.

5 Stir any remaining coffee mixture into the remaining cheese and spoon over the top.

6 Sprinkle with grated chocolate. Serve immediately or chill until required.

MASCARPONE CHEESE

An Italian soft cream cheese made from cow's milk. It has a rich, silky smooth texture and a deliciously creamy flavour. It can be eaten as it is with fresh fruits or flavoured with coffee or chocolate. I usually lighten it slightly by mixing it with an equal quantity of fromage frais or natural thick yogurt.

STEP 1

STEP 3

STEP 5

STEP 6

LIME MOUSSE WITH MANGO

Lime-flavoured cream moulds, served with a fresh mango and lime sauce, make a stunning dessert.

SERVES: 4
PREPARATION: 15 MINS

250 g/8 oz/1 cup fromage frais
grated rind of 1 lime
1 tbsp caster (superfine) sugar
120 ml/4 fl oz/½ cup double (heavy) cream

MANGO SAUCE:
1 mango
juice of 1 lime
4 tsp caster (superfine) sugar

TO DECORATE:
4 cape gooseberries
strips of lime rind

1 Put the fromage frais, lime rind and sugar in a bowl and mix together.

2 Whip the cream and fold into the fromage frais.

3 Line 4 decorative moulds or ramekin dishes with muslin (cheesecloth) or clingfilm (plastic wrap) and divide the mixture evenly among them. Fold the muslin (cheesecloth) over the top and press down firmly.

4 To make the sauce, slice through the mango on each side of the large

flat stone, then cut the flesh from the stone. Remove the skin.

5 Cut off 12 thin slices and set aside. Chop the remaining mango and put into a food processor or blender with the lime juice and sugar. Blend until smooth. Alternatively, push the mango through a non-metallic sieve (strainer) then mix with the lime juice and sugar.

6 Turn out the moulds on to serving plates. Arrange 3 slices of mango on each plate, pour some sauce around and decorate with cape gooseberries and lime rind.

CAPE GOOSEBERRIES

Also known as physalis, cape gooseberries have a tart and mildly scented flavour and make an excellent decoration for many desserts. Peel back the papery husks to expose the bright orange fruits.

STEP 1

STEP 2

STEP 3

STEP 4

BRANDY MOCHA CUPS

A very rich and delicious chocolate dessert that literally takes minutes to make, although you do have to wait for it to set.

SERVES: 4
PREPARATION: 8 MINS,
  CHILLING: 30 MINS

250 ml/ 8 fl oz/ 1 cup double (heavy) cream
1 tsp coffee granules
125 g/ 4 oz dark chocolate, broken into
  pieces
2 tbsp brandy
75 ml/ 3 fl oz/ ¹/₃ cup double (heavy) cream
chocolate curls to decorate
amaretti biscuits (cookies) to serve

1 Put the cream, coffee and chocolate into a saucepan and heat gently, stirring occasionally, until the chocolate has melted.

2 Add the brandy and stir well until it is completely smooth. Remove from the heat and leave to cool.

3 Pour into 4 individual glass dishes and chill until set.

4 Pile a spoonful of cream on to each cup, decorate with chocolate curls and serve with amaretti biscuits (cookies).

VARIATIONS

You can use all kinds of flavourings in this dessert. Try replacing the brandy with almond liqueur to reflect the flavour of the amaretti biscuits (cookies), or use cherry brandy, orange liqueur or, for a non-alcoholic version, orange juice and a little grated orange rind.

CHOCOLATE CURLS

Use a vegetable peeler to scrape curls directly off the edge of a block of chocolate. The chocolate should be at room temperature; if it is too cold the curls will break into small pieces.

STEP 1

STEP 2

STEP 4

STEP 5

STRAWBERRIES ROMANOFF

It is best not to wash strawberries but if it is necessary, do so before you hull them, so that water does not get into the fruit and spoil the flavour.

SERVES: 4
PREPARATION: 15 MINS

300 ml/¹/₂ pint/ 1¹/₄ cups whipping (heavy) cream
2 tbsp orange liqueur
350 g/ 12 oz strawberries, hulled
1 egg white
30 g/ 1 oz/ 2 tbsp caster (superfine) sugar
strawberry leaves to decorate

1 Put the cream and liqueur in a bowl and whip until the cream holds its shape.

2 Put half the strawberries in a food processor and blend to a purée. Alternatively, press through a non-metallic sieve (strainer). Halve the remaining strawberries.

3 Whisk the egg white until stiff then whisk in the sugar. Carefully fold into the cream.

4 Set aside a few strawberry halves for decoration. Fold the remaining halves into the cream mixture with the purée, swirling the mixture to form an attractive marbled effect.

5 Spoon into sundae glasses, decorate with the reserved strawberries and strawberry leaves and serve.

FOLDING

When folding the egg white into the cream use a large metal spoon so that you do not knock out too much air. When you fold in the strawberry purée, stop when it looks nicely marbled.

AMARETTI FIGS WITH RASPBERRY COULIS

Luscious figs served with an almond-flavoured cream and arranged on a pool of fresh raspberry sauce.

STEP 2

Serves: 4
Preparation: 15 mins

120 ml/4 fl oz/½ cup double (heavy) cream
4 amaretti biscuits (cookies)
4 figs
175 g/6 oz raspberries
2 tbsp icing (confectioners') sugar, sifted
raspberry leaves to decorate

1 Set aside 1 tablespoon of the double (heavy) cream then lightly whip the remainder until stiff enough to hold its shape.

2 Put the amaretti biscuits in a plastic bag and crush with a rolling pin until they form fine crumbs. Fold into the whipped cream.

3 Slice each fig into 6 pieces and arrange on 4 serving plates. Put a spoonful of the amaretti cream in the centre of each plate.

4 Press the raspberries through a non-metallic sieve (strainer) then stir in the icing (confectioners') sugar.

5 Spoon the raspberry sauce around the figs and amaretti cream.

6 Put drops of the reserved cream on to the sauce and drag a skewer through the drops to make an attractive pattern. Decorate with raspberry leaves and serve.

STEP 3

RASPBERRY COULIS

The raspberries can be puréed in a food processor if preferred, but they should still be passed through a sieve (strainer) to remove the seeds. Be sure to use a non-metallic sieve (strainer) as metal ones react with the acid in the raspberries and may taint the flavour.

STEP 4

FIGS

There are several varieties of fig; some are pale green, others are gold and some are a luscious deep purple. The skin encloses soft, pink flesh which has a wonderful texture and delicate flavour. Some people prefer to peel figs although they look more attractive if the skin is left on for serving.

STEP 5

STEP 1

STEP 2

STEP 3

STEP 4

WARM CURRANTS IN CASSIS

Crème de cassis is a blackcurrant-based liqueur which comes from France. It is an excellent flavouring for all kinds of fruit dishes, particularly those made with red fruit.

SERVES: **4**
PREPARATION: **15 MINS,**
  COOKING: **10 MINS**

350 g/12 oz blackcurrants
250 g/8 oz redcurrants
6 tbsp caster (superfine) sugar
grated rind and juice of 1 orange
2 tsp arrowroot
2 tbsp crème de cassis
blackcurrant leaves to decorate
whipped cream to serve

1 Using a fork, strip the currants from their stalks and put in a saucepan.

2 Add the sugar and orange rind and juice and heat gently until the sugar has dissolved. Bring to the boil and simmer gently for 5 minutes.

3 Drain the currants, reserving the juice, and put in a bowl. Return the juice to the pan. Mix the arrowroot with a little water and stir into the juice. Bring to the boil, stirring until thickened.

4 Leave to cool slightly then stir in the cassis.

5 Divide the currants among individual serving dishes and pour over the sauce. Decorate with blackcurrant leaves and serve with whipped cream.

VARIATION

If you don't have any crème de cassis you could use port or an orange-flavoured liqueur instead.

CURRANTS

Be careful not to overcook the currants or they will become mushy.

QUICK & EASY INGREDIENTS

Sweet & Sour Red Cabbage

SERVES 4:

750 g/1¹/₂ lb red cabbage,
  shredded
2 tbsp wine vinegar
1 tbsp brown sugar
salt and pepper

1. Cook the cabbage in boiling salted water for 5 minutes. Drain well, reserving 2 tbsp of the cooking liquid.
2. Return the cabbage and reserved liquid to the pan and add the vinegar, sugar and seasoning. Heat gently to warm through.

Cabbage With Ginger

SERVES 4:

2 tbsp sunflower oil
2 garlic cloves, chopped
2.5 cm/1 inch piece ginger root,
  chopped
500 g/1 lb Savoy cabbage,
  shredded
4 tbsp water
1 tbsp dark soy sauce
1 tsp sesame oil
salt and pepper

1. Heat the oil in a frying pan (skillet) and stir-fry the garlic and ginger for 30 seconds.
2. Add the cabbage and stir-fry for 3 minutes. Add the water and seasoning and stir-fry for 3 minutes until tender but still slightly crisp.
3. Stir in the soy sauce and sesame oil and serve immediately.

We live in an age when almost every magazine we pick up shows us new ways of enjoying home-cooked food and urges us to experiment in the kitchen with new ingredients and cooking techniques. However, such are the demands on our time that the labour-saving aspects of convenience foods are often preferred to the freshness and quality of home cooking. This does not have to be the case. Most supermarkets now have delicatessens and wet-fish counters providing selections of ready-prepared food – skinned, filleted, chopped and washed – which all cut down on time in the kitchen. Good planning of store-cupboard ingredients also means you can produce a meal at a moment's notice.

The following suggestions include the items I find most useful to have in my kitchen.

REFRIGERATOR FOODS

Yogurt
Thick natural yogurt is useful for serving as an instant dessert with brown sugar or honey. It is also useful as a low-fat alternative to cream and can be stirred into sauces instead of cream, but don't allow the sauce to boil.

Lemons
A squeeze of fresh lemon can liven up grilled (broiled) or poached fish, perk up a salad dressing or a sauce or prevent avocados or sliced fruits from discolouring.

Apricot compôte
Thick chunks of apricots stewed in natural juices and lightly sweetened. A good dollop spooned into a bowl of yogurt forms part of my daily breakfast. It is also excellent as a filling for tarts or topped with crunchy fried breadcrumbs and toasted nuts.

Parmesan cheese
Buy in a single piece and keep in the refrigerator to be grated when you need it – this will give a much better flavour than ready-grated Parmesan. Use a vegetable peeler to make Parmesan shavings.

Cheddar cheese
Always a useful, tasty standby for sauces, salads, sandwiches and grilled (broiled) toppings.

Streaky bacon
A few crisply fried bacon slices perk up an avocado salad, make a delicious sandwich with lettuce and tomato or add flavour to vegetable soup.

Free-range eggs
These come from birds which have the freedom to roam at will. In my opinion, these eggs have a much better flavour.

Mayonnaise
To add to sandwich fillings, sauces or dips. Mix with a spoonful of thick natural yogurt and a handful of chopped herbs to make a quick dressing for a potato salad.

THE STORE CUPBOARD

Dried, canned and preserved foods are ideal for making a quick meal and should always be kept to hand. They keep well in a cool, dark cupboard, but remember that nothing lasts indefinitely, so be sure to rotate the ingredients of your store cupboard and keep a check on the use-by dates of the goods.

Dried pasta

Keep a selection such as spaghetti, tagliatelle and, if you can find it, papardelle – a wider variety of tagliatelle. Shell-shaped conchiglie, spiral-shaped fusilli and bow-shaped farfalle are good for holding sauces.

Basmati rice

Basmati rice has a distinctive fragrant aroma and flavour and is the quickest rice to cook; it only takes 8 minutes.

Chinese egg noodles

These vary in size; thread noodles are the quickest to use because they only need to be soaked in boiling salted water for 3 minutes before serving.

Couscous and bulgur wheat

These grains are both very quick to use as they have been partially pre-cooked. Simply soak for 5 minutes in boiling water then drain and serve.

Canned pulses

Pinto, haricot (navy), flageolet (small navy), cannellini and red kidney beans are all excellent, either in salads or casseroles. Drain and rinse before use.

Canned tomatoes

The most useful of all canned products; quicker to prepare than fresh tomatoes and often having more flavour than the poor-quality tomatoes available in the winter. Chopped canned tomatoes are best, and are often sold with added flavourings such as chilli or herbs.

Sun-dried tomatoes

Drying tomatoes in the sun concentrates their flavour. Most are sold in jars of olive oil which keeps them moist. They have a fantastic flavour and are delicious to eat straight from the jar with a hunk of bread. Sun-dried tomatoes enliven pasta, rice or tomato sauces and give them great depth of flavour. I use the oil from the jar to make a tomato vinaigrette dressing (see page 78).

Sun-dried tomato paste

This is a pesto-like sauce made from puréed sun-dried tomatoes which are mixed with olive oil, balsamic vinegar and herbs.

Black olive paste

The black olive paste I use is made with finely chopped Greek kalamata olives which have been mixed with olive oil and herbs. I use it in dressings or spread it on pizza bases or on ciabatta bread. A paste made from green olives is also available.

Pesto sauce

The basic ingredients of pesto sauce are basil, Parmesan cheese and pine kernels (nuts), bound together with olive oil. It is useful as a flavouring for soups and dressings or tossed into fresh pasta.

Courgettes (Zucchini) With Herbs

SERVES 4:

500 g/1 lb courgettes (zucchini), sliced
15 g/¹/₂ oz/1 tbsp butter
1 tsp chopped fresh tarragon
1 tsp chopped fresh thyme
1 tbsp chopped fresh parsley
salt and pepper

1. Cook the courgettes (zucchini) in boiling salted water for 5 minutes until tender. Drain thoroughly.
2. Put the butter and herbs in the saucepan, heat gently until the butter has melted then add the courgettes (zucchini) and seasoning to taste and toss together.

Cucumber With Dill

SERVES 4:

1¹/₂ cucumbers, peeled
15 g/¹/₂ oz/1 tbsp butter
2 tsp chopped fresh dill
salt and pepper

1. Cut the cucumber into 1 x 5 cm/¹/₂ x 2¹/₂ inch fingers. Put into a saucepan of boiling salted water, bring back to the boil and simmer for 5 minutes until just tender. Drain thoroughly.
2. Melt the butter in the pan, add the cucumber, dill and seasoning and shake over a moderate heat for 1–2 minutes until heated through.

Tomato Sauce

MAKES 350 ML/12 FL OZ/
1¹/₂ CUPS:
2 tbsp olive oil
1 onion, chopped
1 garlic clove, chopped
425 g/14 oz can chopped
*   tomatoes*
1 tbsp tomato purée (paste)
120 ml/4 fl oz/¹/₂ cup stock
1 fresh bay leaf
salt and pepper

Heat the oil in a saucepan and
fry the onion until softened.
Add the remaining ingredients,
cover and simmer for 10
minutes, stirring occasionally.
   If you prefer a smooth sauce,
blend in a food processor or
blender or press through a
sieve (strainer).

Tomato Vinaigrette Dressing
A good dressing for tomato
based salads or bean salads.

MAKES 250 ML/8 FL OZ/
1 CUP:
120 ml/4 fl oz/¹/₂ cup oil from a
*   jar of sun-dried tomatoes*
3 tbsp red wine vinegar
1 garlic clove, crushed
1 tbsp chopped fresh basil
1 tbsp tomato purée (paste)
1 tsp Dijon mustard
1 tsp clear honey
salt and pepper

Put all the ingredients into a
screw-top jar and shake
vigorously.

Soy sauce
An invaluable seasoning for Chinese stir-
fries, but can also add flavour to all kinds
of savoury dishes.

Sesame oil
Sesame oil is made from toasted sesame
seeds. It gives a delicious nutty flavour to
stir-fries.

Sunflower oil
A good general-purpose oil, best used
when you don't want to overpower the
food with a strong flavour such as that of
olive oil.

Olive oil
Olive oil is an essential ingredient in
many dishes and is best when used
liberally in Mediterranean food. A cold
pressed, fruity, extra virgin oil enhances
the flavour of almost any dish.

Balsamic vinegar
The mellow richness of this vinegar adds
a new dimension to salads, pulses and
stir-fried vegetables, and a few drops over
strawberries is a surprising but delightful
combination.

Wine vinegar
Wine vinegar is invaluable for dressings.
White wine vinegar is more versatile, but
if you have room, keep a red wine
vinegar and a flavoured one too, such as
raspberry or sherry vinegar.

Olives
Both black and green olives are excellent
for adding to salads, stews, pizzas and
nibbles. When buying black olives, look
for unpitted ones, preferably the purple-
brown kalamata olives from Greece.

Capers
I use capers to add a piquant tang to
salads, vegetables or fish sauces.

Chilli, coriander (cilantro), ginger & garlic pastes
These herbs and spices can be bought in
small jars. They are convenient and
quick to use but don't have as good a
flavour as the fresh equivalents. Store in
the refrigerator once opened and used
within 3 weeks.

Spices
Spices give exotic flavours to foods and
can be varied according to your taste.
The spices I use most frequently are
paprika, ground ginger, cumin,
coriander, chilli and cardamom. Store in
a cool, dark place and buy spices in small
quantities only as they deteriorate over
time. To get the most aromatic flavours
from spices, grind your own in a pestle
and mortar or use a spice grinder.

Black peppercorns
Can be used in just about all savoury
dishes. Grind them in a pepper mill when
needed, to get the full aromatic flavour.

Coconut powder and creamed coconut
These are very useful for Thai and Indian
dishes. As well as giving flavour, they
also improve the texture of sauces, giving
them a rich smoothness. Creamed
coconut is sold in blocks and is best
grated or finely chopped before being
added to dishes.

Mustard

French mustards such as Dijon and Meaux are the ones I use most frequently because they are milder than English mustard. Meaux mustard is a type of wholegrain mustard and contains whole mustard seeds.

Nuts

Almonds, hazelnuts and pine kernels (nuts) are great to sprinkle over salads, stir-fries and puddings. I always toast them first to intensify their flavour.

Dried apricots and prunes

Delicious to nibble as they are, but when cooked in apple juice for 15 minutes, sprinkled with toasted nuts and served with yogurt, they make an excellent quick pudding.

Honey

Choose a clear honey with a good flavour, such as heather or orange blossom. Honey is ideal for an instant pudding drizzled over natural yogurt.

Chocolate

Use chocolate to make a sauce to cheer up the vanilla ice cream in the freezer. Just melt with a little water and some sugar and boil for a few minutes. Serve hot, poured over the ice cream.

Amaretti biscuits (cookies)

These almond biscuits (cookies) from Italy are very useful to give an instant almond flavour and crunchy texture to desserts. Crush them and add to whipped cream, or mix them with melted butter for a crumb base or topping.

Soft brown sugar

This is good when sprinkled over fromage frais or spooned over sliced bananas and then grilled (broiled) until caramelized.

Vanilla pod (bean)

Keep a vanilla pod (bean) in a jar of caster (superfine) sugar. It will flavour the sugar quite quickly and the sugar can then be used to add flavour to custards or mousses. A vanilla pod (bean) can also be used to flavour milk that is to be used in custards, etc. Heat the milk gently then leave to infuse for 30 minutes. Rinse and dry the vanilla pod (bean) and keep it to be used again.

Brandy, rum and liqueurs

I use these mostly to enhance sauces, both sweet and savoury, but they are excellent when whipped into sweetened cream to serve with fresh fruit.

FRESH HERBS

Fresh herbs are an essential part of my cooking. They add such freshness and flavour and most are far superior to their dried equivalents.

Supermarkets now sell herbs growing in small pots, which can be kept on the kitchen window sill. However, growing a few herbs in the garden or a window-box can add another dimension to the pleasure of cooking. Parsley, coriander (cilantro), basil, mint and chives are particularly worthwhile. Hang a few twigs of bay leaves in your kitchen as they are so useful for flavouring kebabs, marinades, sauces and stews.

Banana Raita

SERVES 4:
1 ripe banana, sliced
150 ml/¹/₄ pint/²/₃ cup natural
 yogurt
salt and pepper

Gently mix together all the ingredients and serve immediately.

Onion Relish

SERVES 4:
1 onion, chopped
2 tomatoes, peeled and chopped
1 tsp chopped fresh red chilli
1¹/₂ tbsp lemon juice
2 tbsp chopped fresh coriander
 (cilantro)
salt and pepper

Mix together all the ingredients and serve or chill until required.

INDEX